Thomas Bailey Aldrich

Flower and Thorn Later Poems

Thomas Bailey Aldrich

Flower and Thorn Later Poems

ISBN/EAN: 9783743328488

Manufactured in Europe, USA, Canada, Australia, Japa

Cover: Foto ©Thomas Meinert / pixelio.de

Manufactured and distributed by brebook publishing software (www.brebook.com)

Thomas Bailey Aldrich

Flower and Thorn Later Poems

CONTENTS.

I.

SPRING IN NEW ENGLAND.

	Page
Spring in New England	13

II.

MIANTOWONA.

Miantowona	25

III.

THE LEGEND OF ARA-CŒLI.

The Legend of Ara-Cœli	39

IV.

INTERLUDES.

Destiny	65
Unsung	66
Frost-Work	68
Rococo	69
Landscape	70
Identity	71
Nocturne	72
A Snow-Flake	73

CONTENTS.

Across the Street	74
Rencontre	76
An Untimely Thought	77
Rondeau	79
Latakia	80
A Winter-Piece	82
Quatrains:	
Day and Night	83
Maple Leaves	83
A Child's Grave	84
Pessimist and Optimist	84
Grace and Strength	84
Among the Pines	85
From the Spanish	85
Moonrise at Sea	85
Masks	86
Coquette	86
Epitaphs	86
Popularity	87
Human Ignorance	87
Spendthrift	87
The Iron Age	88
On reading ——	88
The Rose	88
From Eastern Sources	89
The Parcæ	90
Fable	91
Palinode	93

V.

THE FLIGHT OF THE GODDESS, Etc.

The Flight of the Goddess	97
On an Intaglio Head of Minerva	101

The Guerdon	105
Lost at Sea	109
An Old Castle	112
In an Atelier	116
The World's Way	121
Tita's Tears	123
The King's Wine	127
Dirge	129
The Piazza of St. Mark at Midnight	132
Thorwaldsen	134

VI.

SONNETS.

"Touched with the delicate green of early May"	137
"Thus spake his dust, so seemed it as I read"	138
"Herewith I send you three pressed withered flowers"	139
"Stand here and look, and softly hold your breath"	140
"You by the Arno shape your marble dream"	141
"While men pay reverence to mighty things"	142
"Enamored architect of airy rhyme"	143
"They never crowned him, never knew his worth"	144
"In scarlet clusters o'er the gray stone-wall"	145
"Yonder we see it from the steamer's deck"	146
"While yet my lip was breathing youth's first breath"	147
"When to soft Sleep we give ourselves away"	148

I.

SPRING IN NEW ENGLAND.

SPRING IN NEW ENGLAND.

I.

THE long years come and go,
    And the Past,
The sorrowful, splendid Past,
With its glory and its woe,
    Seems never to have been.
The bugle's taunting blast
Has died away by Southern ford and glen:
The mock-bird sings unfrightened in its dell;
The ensanguined stream flows pure again;
Where once the hissing death-bolt fell,
And all along the artillery's level lines
    Leapt flames of hell,
The farmer smiles upon the sprouting grain,
    And tends his vines.

Seems never to have been?
   O sombre days and grand,
      How ye crowd back once more,
Seeing our heroes' graves are green
   By the Potomac and the Cumberland,
      And in the valley of the Shenandoah!

II.

Now while the pale arbutus in our woods
Wakes to faint life beneath the dead year's leaves,
And the bleak North lets loose its wailing broods
Of winds upon us, and the gray sea grieves
Along our coast; while yet the Winter's hand
Heavily presses on New England's heart,
And Spring averts the sunshine of her eyes
Lest some vain cowslip should untimely start —
While we are housed in this rude season's gloom,
   In this rude land,
      Bereft of warmth and bloom,
We know, far off beneath the Southern skies,
Where the flush blossoms mock our drifts of snow

And the lithe vine unfolds its emerald sheen —
On many a sunny hillside there, we know
    Our heroes' graves are green.

III.

  The long years come, but *they*
    Come not again!
  Through vapors dense and gray
    Steals back the May,
  But they come not again —
    Swept by the battle's fiery breath
    Down unknown ways of death.
How can our fancies help but go
Out from this realm of mist and rain,
Out from this realm of sleet and snow,
When the first Southern violets blow?

IV.

  While yet the year is young
  Many a garland shall be hung
    In our gardens of the dead;

On obelisk and urn
Shall the lilac's purple burn,
  And the wild-rose leaves be shed.
And afar in the woodland ways,
Through the rustic church-yard gate
Matrons and maidens shall pass,
Striplings and white-haired men,
And, spreading aside the grass,
Linger at name and date,
Remembering old, old days!
And the lettering on each stone
Where the mould's green breath has blown
Tears shall wash clear again!

V.

But far away to the South, in the sultry, stricken land —
On the banks of silvery streams gurgling among their reeds,
By many a drear morass, where the long-necked pelican feeds,
By many a dark bayou, and blinding dune of sand,

By many a cypress swamp where the cayman seeks its
 prey,
In many a moss-hung wood, the twilight's haunt by day,
And down where the land's parched lip drinks at the
 salt sea-waves,
And the ghostly sails glide by — there are piteous nameless graves.

  Their names no tongue may tell,
  Buried there where they fell,
  The bravest of our braves!
  Never sweetheart, or friend,
   Wan pale mother, or bride,
  Over these mounds shall bend,
   Tenderly putting aside
  The unremembering grass!
   Never the votive wreath
   For the unknown brows beneath,
  Never a tear, alas!
  How can our fancies help but go
  Out from this realm of mist and rain,

Out from this realm of sleet and snow,
When the first Southern violets blow?
How must our thought bend over them,
Blessing the flowers that cover them —
    Piteous, nameless graves!

VI.

Ah, but the life they gave
Is not shut in the grave:
The valorous spirits freed
Live in the vital deed!
Marble shall crumble to dust,
Plinth of bronze and of stone,
Carved escutcheon and crest —
Silently, one by one,
The sculptured lilies fall:
Softly the tooth of the rust
Gnaws through the brazen shield:
Broken, and covered with stains,
The crossed stone swords must yield:
Mined by the frost and the drouth,

Smitten by north and south,
Smitten by east and west,
Down comes column and all!
But the great deed remains.

VII.

When we remember how they died —
In dark ravine and on the mountain-side,
In leaguered fort and fire-encircled town,
Upon the gun-boat's splintered deck,
And where the iron ships went down —
How their dear lives were spent,
In the crushed and reddened wreck,
By lone lagoons and streams,
In the weary hospital-tent,
In the cockpit's crowded hive —
How they languished and died
In the black stockades — it seems
Ignoble to be alive!
Tears will well to our eyes,
And the bitter doubt will rise —

But hush! for the strife is done,
Forgiven are wound and scar;
The fight was fought and won
Long since, on sea and shore,
And every scattered star
Set in the blue once more:
We are one as before,
With the blot from our scutcheon gone!

VIII.

So let our heroes rest
Upon your sunny breast:
Keep them, O South, our tender hearts and true,
Keep them, O South, and learn to hold them dear
From year to year!
Never forget,
Dying for us, they died for you.
This hallowed dust should knit us closer yet.

IX.

Hark! 't is the bluebird's venturous strain
  High on the old fringed elm at the gate —
    Sweet-voiced, valiant on the swaying bough,
      Alert, elate,
  Dodging the fitful spits of snow,
  New England's poet-laureate
Telling us Spring has come again!

II.

MIANTOWONA.

MIANTOWONA.

I.

LONG ere the Pale Face
 Crossed the Great Water,
Miantowona
Passed, with her beauty,
Into a legend
Pure as a wild-flower
Found in a broken
Ledge by the seaside.

Let us revere them —
These wildwood legends,
Born of the camp-fire.
Let them be handed
Down to our children —

Richest of heirlooms.

No land may claim them:

They are ours only,

Like our grand rivers,

Like our vast prairies,

Like our dead heroes.

II.

In the pine-forest,
Guarded by shadows,
Lieth the haunted
Pond of the Red Men.
Ringed by the emerald
Mountains, it lies there
Like an untarnished
Buckler of silver,
Dropped in that valley
By the Great Spirit!
Weird are the figures
Traced on its margins —
Vine-work and leaf-work,
Down-drooping fuchsias,
Knots of sword-grasses,
Moonlight and starlight,

Clouds scudding northward.

Sometimes an eagle

Flutters across it;

Sometimes a single

Star on its bosom

Nestles till morning.

Far in the ages,

Miantowona,

Rose of the Hurons,

Came to these waters.

Where the dank greensward

Slopes to the pebbles,

Miantowona

Sat in her anguish.

Ice to her maidens,

Ice to the chieftains,

Fire to her lover!

Here he had won her,

Here they had parted,

Here could her tears flow.

With unwet eyelash,
Miantowona
Nursed her old father,
Gray-eyed Tawanda,
Oldest of Hurons,
Soothed his complainings,
Smiled when he chid her
Vaguely for nothing —
He was so weak now,
Like a shrunk cedar
White with the hoar-frost.
Sometimes she gently
Linked arms with maidens,
Joined in their dances:
Not with her people,
Not in the wigwam,
Wept for her lover.

Ah! who was like him?
Fleet as an arrow,
Strong as a bison,

Lithe as a panther,
Soft as the south-wind,
Who was like Wawah?
There is one other
Stronger and fleeter,
Bearing no wampum,
Wearing no war-paint,
Ruler of councils,
Chief of the war-path —
Who can gainsay him,
Who can defy him?
His is the lightning,
His is the whirlwind,
Let us be humble,
We are but ashes —
'T is the Great Spirit!

Ever at nightfall
Miantowona
Strayed from the lodges,
Passed through the shadows

Into the forest:
There by the pond-side
Spread her black tresses
Over her forehead.

Sad is the loon's cry
Heard in the twilight;
Sad is the night-wind,
Moaning and moaning;
Sadder the stifled
Sob of a widow.

Low on the pebbles
Murmured the water:
Often she fancied
It was young Wawah
Playing the reed-flute.
Sometimes a dry branch
Snapped in the forest:
Then she rose, startled,
Ruddy as sunrise,
Warm for his coming!

But when he came not,
Back through the darkness,
Half broken-hearted,
Miantowona
Went to her people.

When an old oak dies,
First 't is the tree-tops,
Then the low branches,
Then the gaunt stem goes:
So fell Tawanda,
Oldest of Hurons,
Chief of the chieftains.

Miantowona
Wept not, but softly
Closed the sad eyelids;
With her own fingers
Fastened the deer-skin
Over his shoulders;
Then laid beside him

Ash-bow and arrows,
Pipe-bowl and wampum,
Dried corn and bear-meat —
All that was needful
On the long journey.
Thus old Tawanda,
Went to the hunting
Grounds of the Red Man.

Then, as the dirges
Rose from the village,
Miantowona
Stole from the mourners,
Stole through the cornfields,
Passed like a phantom
Into the shadows
Through the pine-forest.

One who had watched her —
It was Nahoho,
Loving her vainly —

Saw, as she passed him,
That in her features
Made his stout heart quail.
He could but follow.
Quick were her footsteps,
Light as a snow-flake,
Leaving no traces
On the white clover.

Like a trained runner,
Winner of prizes,
Into the woodlands
Plunged the young chieftain.
Once he abruptly
Halted, and listened;
Then he sped forward
Faster and faster
Toward the bright water.
Breathless he reached it.
Why did he crouch then,
Stark as a statue?

What did he see there
Could so appall him?
Only a circle
Swiftly expanding,
Fading before him;
But, as he watched it,
Up from the centre,
Slowly, superbly
Rose a Pond-Lily.

One cry of wonder,
Shrill as the loon's call,
Rang through the forest,
Startling the silence,
Startling the mourners
Chanting the death-song.
Forth from the village,
Flocking together
Came all the Hurons —
Striplings and warriors,
Maidens and old men,
Squaws with pappooses.

No word was spoken:
There stood the Hurons
On the dank greensward,
With their swart faces
Bowed in the twilight.
What did they see there?
Only a Lily
Rocked on the azure
Breast of the water.

Then they turned sadly
Each to the other,
Tenderly murmuring,
"Miantowona!"
Soft as the dew falls
Down through the midnight,
Cleaving the starlight,
Echo repeated,
"Miantowona!"

III.

THE LEGEND OF ARA-CŒLI.

THE LEGEND OF ARA-CŒLI.

I.

LOOKING at Fra Gervasio,
    Wrinkled and withered and old and gray,
A dry Franciscan from crown to toe,
You would never imagine, by any chance,
That, in the convent garden one day,
He spun this thread of golden romance.

Romance to me, but to him, indeed,
'T was a matter that did not hold a doubt;
A miracle, nothing more nor less.
Did I think it strange that, in our need,
Leaning from Heaven to our distress,
The Virgin brought such things about —
Gave mute things speech, made dead things move? —
Mother of Mercy, Lady of Love!

Besides, I might, if I wished, behold
The Bambino's self in his cloth of gold
And silver tissue, lying in state
In the Sacristy. Would the signor wait?

Whoever will go to Rome may see,
In the chapel of the Sacristy
Of Ara-Cœli, the Sainted Child —
Garnished from throat to foot with rings
And brooches and precious offerings,
And its little nose kissed quite away
By dying lips. At Epiphany,
If the holy winter day prove mild,
It is shown to the wondering, gaping crowd
On the church's steps — held high aloft —
While every sinful head is bowed,
And the music plays, and the censers' soft
White breath ascends like silent prayer.

Many a beggar kneeling there,
Tattered and hungry, without a home,

Would not envy the Pope of Rome,
If he, the beggar, had half the care
Bestowed on *him* that falls to the share
Of yonder Image — for you must know
It has its minions to come and go,
Its perfumed chamber, remote and still,
Its silken couch, and its jewelled throne,
And a special carriage of its own
To take the air in, when it will.
And though it may neither drink nor eat,
By a nod to its ghostly seneschal
It could have of the choicest wine and meat.
Often some princess, brown and tall,
Comes, and unclasping from her arm
The glittering bracelet, leaves it, warm
With her throbbing pulse, at the Baby's feet.
Ah, he is loved by high and low,
Adored alike by simple and wise.
The people kneel to him in the street.
What a felicitous lot is his —
To lie in the light of ladies' eyes,

Petted and pampered, and never to know
The want of a dozen *soldi* or so!
And what does he do for all of this?
What does the little Bambino do?
It cures the sick, and, in fact, 't is said
Can almost bring life back to the dead.
Who doubts it? Not Fra Gervasio.
When one falls ill, it is left alone
For a while with one — and the fever's gone!

At least, 't was once so; but to-day
It is never permitted, unattended
By monk or priest, to work its lure
At sick folks' beds — all that was ended
By one poor soul whose feeble clay
Satan tempted and made secure.

It was touching this very point the friar
Told me the legend, that afternoon,
In the cloisteral garden all on fire
With scarlet poppies and golden stalks.

Here and there on the sunny walks,
Startled by some slight sound we made,
A lizard, awaking from its swoon,
Shot like an arrow into the shade.
I can hear the fountain's languorous tune,
(How it comes back, that hour in June
When just to exist was joy enough!)
I can see the olives, silvery-gray,
The carven masonry rich with stains,
The gothic windows with lead-set panes,
The flag-paved cortile, the convent grates,
And Fra Gervasio holding his snuff
In a squirrel-like, meditative way
'Twixt finger and thumb. But the Legend waits.

II.

It was long ago (so long ago
That Fra Gervasio did not know
What year of our Lord), there came to Rome
Across the Campagna's flaming red,
A certain Filippo and his wife —
Peasants, and very newly wed.
In the happy spring and blossom of life,
When the light heart chirrups to lovers' calls,
These two, like a pair of birds, had come
And built their nest 'gainst the city's walls.

He, with his scanty garden-plots,
Raised flowers and fruit for the market-place,
Where she, with her pensile, flower-like face —
Own sister to her forget-me-nots —
Played merchant: and so they thrived apace,
In humble content, with humble cares

And modest longings, till, unawares,
Sorrow crept on them; for to their nest
Had come no little ones, and at last,
When six or seven summers had past,
Seeing no baby at her breast,
The husband brooded, and then grew cold;
Scolded and fretted over this —
Who would tend them when they were old,
And palsied, maybe, sitting alone,
Hungry, beside the cold hearth-stone?
Not to have children, like the rest!
It cankered the very heart of bliss.

Then he fell into indolent ways,
Neglecting the garden for days and days,
Playing at *mora*, drinking wine,
With this and that one — letting the vine
Run riot and die for want of care,
And the choke-weeds gather; for it was spring,
When everything needed nurturing.
But he would drowse for hours in the sun,

Or sit on the broken step by the shed,
Like a man whose honest toil is done,
Sullen, with never a word to spare,
Or a word that were better all unsaid.

And Nina, so light of thought before,
Singing about the cottage door
In her mountain dialect — sang no more;
But came and went, sad-faced and shy,
Wishing, at times, that she might die,
Brooding and fretting in her turn.
Often, in passing along the street,
Her basket of flowers poised, peasant-wise,
On a lustrous braided coil of her hair,
She would halt, and her dusky cheek would burn
Like a poppy, beholding at her feet
Some stray little urchin, dirty and bare.
And sudden tears would spring to her eyes
That the tiny waif was not her own,
To fondle, and kiss, and teach to pray.
Then she passed onward, making moan.

Sometimes she would stand in the sunny square,
Like a slim bronze statue of Despair,
Watching the children at their play.

In the broad piazza was a shrine,
With Our Lady holding on her knee
A small nude waxen effigy.
Nina passed by it every day,
And morn and even, in rain or shine,
Repeated an *ave* there. " Divine
Mother," she 'd cry, as she turned away,
" Sitting in paradise, undefiled,
O, have pity on my distress ! "
Then glancing back at the rosy Child,
She would cry to it, in her helplessness,
" Pray her to send the like to me ! "

Now once as she knelt before the saint,
Lifting her hands in silent plain,
She paled, and her heavy heart grew faint
At a thought which flashed across her brain—

The blinding thought that, perhaps if she
Had lived in the world's miraculous morn,
God might have chosen *her* to be
The mother — O heavenly ecstasy! —
Of the little babe in the manger born!
She, too, was a peasant girl, like her,
The wife of the lowly carpenter!
Like Joseph's wife, a peasant girl!

Her strange little head was in a whirl
As she rose from her knees to wander home,
Leaving her basket at the shrine;
So dazed was she, she scarcely knew
The old familiar streets of Rome,
Nor whither she wished to go, in fine;
But wandered on, now crept, now flew,
In the gathering twilight, till she came
Breathless, bereft of sense and sight,
To the gloomy Arch of Constantine,
And there they found her, late that night,
With her cheeks like snow and her lips like flame!

Many a time from day to day,
She heard, as if in a troubled dream,
Footsteps around her, and some one saying —
Was it Filippo? — "Is she dead?"
Then it was some one near her praying,
And she was drifting — drifting away
From saints and martyrs in endless glory!
She seemed to be floating down a stream,
Yet knew she was lying in her bed.
The fancy held her that she had died,
And this was her soul in purgatory,
Until, one morning, two holy men
From the convent came, and laid at her side
The Bambino. Blessed Virgin! then
Nina looked up, and laughed, and wept,
And folded it close to her heart, and slept.

Slept such a soft, refreshing sleep,
That when she awoke her eyes had taken
That hyaline lustre, dewy, deep,
Of violets when they first awaken;

And the half-unravelled, fragile thread
Of life was knitted together again.
But she shrunk with sudden, strange new pain,
And seemed to droop like a flower, the day
The Capuchins came, with solemn tread,
To carry the Miracle Child away!

III.

ERE spring in the heart of pansies burned,
Or the buttercup had loosed its gold,
Nina was busy as ever of old
With fireside cares; but was not the same,
For from the hour when she had turned
To clasp the Image the fathers brought
To her dying-bed, a single thought
Had taken possession of her brain:
A purpose, as steady as the flame
Of a lamp in some cathedral crypt,
Had lighted her on her bed of pain;
The thirst and the fever, they had slipt
Away like visions, but this had stayed —
To have the Bambino brought again,
To have it, and keep it for her own!

That was the secret dream which made
Life for her now — in the streets, alone,
At night, and morning, and when she prayed.

How should she wrest it from the hand
Of the jealous Church? How keep the Child?
Flee with it into some distant land —
Like mother Mary from Herod's ire?
Ah, well, she knew not; she only knew
It was written down in the Book of Fate
That she should have her heart's desire,
And very soon now, for of late,
In a dream, the little thing had smiled
Up in her face, with one eye's blue
Peering from underneath her breast,
Which the baby fingers had softly prest
Aside, to look at her! Holy one!
But that should happen ere all was done.

Lying dark in the woman's mind —
Unknown, like a seed in fallow ground —

Was the germ of a plan, confused and blind
At first, but which, as the weeks rolled round,
Reached light, and flowered, — a subtile flower,
Deadly as nightshade. In that same hour
She sought the husband and said to him,
With crafty tenderness in her eyes
And treacherous archings of her brows,
"Filippo, mio, thou lov'st me well?
Truly? Then get thee to the house
Of the long-haired Jew Ben Raphaim —
Seller of curious tapestries,
(Ah, he hath everything to sell!)
The cunning carver of images —
And bid him to carve thee to the life
A *bambinetto* like that they gave
In my arms, to hold me from the grave
When the fever pierced me like a knife.
Perhaps, if we set the image there
By the Cross, the saints would hear the prayer
Which in all these years they have not heard."

Then the husband went, without a word,
To the crowded Ghetto; for since the days
Of Nina's illness, the man had been
A tender husband — with lover's ways
Striving, as best he might, to wean
The wife from her sadness, and to bring
Back to the home whence it had fled
The happiness of that laughing spring
When they, like a pair of birds, had wed.

The image! It was a woman's whim —
They were full of whims. But what to him
Were a dozen pieces of silver spent,
If it made her happy? And so he went
To the house of the Jew Ben Raphaim.
And the carver heard, and bowed, and smiled,
And fell to work as if he had known
The thought that lay in the woman's brain,
And somehow taken it for his own:
For even before the month was flown
He had carved a figure so like the Child

Of Ara-Cœli, you'd not have told,
Had both been decked with jewel and chain
And dressed alike in a dress of gold,
Which was the true one of the twain.

When Nina beheld it first, her heart
Stood still with wonder. The skilful Jew
Had given the eyes the tender blue,
And the cheeks the delicate olive hue,
And the form almost the curve and line
Of the Image the good Apostle made
Immortal with his miraculous art,
What time the sculptor[1] dreamed in the shade
Under the skies of Palestine.
The bright new coins that clinked in the palm
Of the carver in wood were blurred and dim
Compared with the eyes that looked at him

---

[1] According to the monastic legend, the *Santissimo Bambino* was carved by a pilgrim, out of a tree which grew on the Mount of Olives, and painted by St. Luke while the pilgrim was sleeping over his work.

From the low sweet brows, so seeming calm;
Then he went his way, and her joy broke free,
And Filippo smiled to hear Nina sing
In the old, old fashion — carolling
Like a very thrush, with many a trill
And long-drawn, flute-like, honeyed note,
Till the birds in the farthest mulberry,
Each outstretching its amber bill,
Answered her with melodious throat.

Thus sped two days; but on the third
Her singing ceased, and there came a change
As of death on Nina; her talk grew strange,
Then she sunk in a trance, nor spoke nor stirred;
And the husband, wringing his hands, dismayed,
Watched by the bed; but she breathed no word
That night, nor until the morning broke,
When she roused from the spell, and feebly laid
Her hand on Filippo's arm, and spoke:
"Quickly, Filippo! get thee gone
To the holy fathers, and beg them send

The Bambino hither"— her cheeks were wan
And her eyes like coals—"O, go, my friend,
Or all is said!" Through the morning's gray
Filippo hurried, like one distraught,
To the monks, and told his tale; and they,
Straight after matins, came and brought
The Miracle Child, and went their way.

Once more in her arms was the Infant laid,
After these weary months, once more!
Yet the woman seemed like a thing of stone
While the dark-robed fathers knelt and prayed;
But the instant the holy friars were gone
She arose, and took the broidered gown
From the Baby Christ, and the yellow crown
And the votive brooches and rings it wore,
Till the little figure, so gay before
In its princely apparel, stood as bare
As your ungloved hand. With tenderest care,
At her feet, 'twixt blanket and counterpane,
She hid the Babe; and then, reaching down

To the coffer wherein the thing had lain,
Drew forth Ben Raphaim's manikin
In haste, and dressed it in robe and crown,
With lace and bawble and diamond-pin.
This finished, she turned to stone again,
And lay as one would have thought quite dead,
If it had not been for a spot of red
Upon either cheek. At the close of day
The Capuchins came, with solemn tread,
And carried the false bambino away!

Over the vast Campagna's plain,
At sunset, a wind began to blow
(From the Apennines it came, they say),
Softly at first, and then to grow —
As the twilight gathered and hurried by —
To a gale, with sudden tumultuous rain
And thunder muttering far away.
When the night was come, from the blackened sky
The spear-tongued lightning slipped like a snake,
And the great clouds clashed, and seemed to shake

The earth to its centre. Then swept down
Such a storm as was never seen in Rome
By any one living in that day.
Not a soul dared venture from his home,
Not a soul in all the crowded town.
Dumb beasts dropped dead, with terror, in stall;
Great chimney-stacks were overthrown,
And about the streets the tiles were blown
Like leaves in autumn. A fearful night,
With ominous voices in the air!
Indeed, it seemed like the end of all.
In the convent, the monks for very fright
Went not to bed, but each in his cell
Counted his beads by the taper's light,
Quaking to hear the dreadful sounds,
And shrivelling in the lightning's glare.
It appeared as if the rivers of Hell
Had risen, and overleaped their bounds.

In the midst of this, at the convent door,
Above the tempest's raving and roar

Came a sudden knocking! Mother of Grace,
What desperate wretch was forced to face
Such a night as that was out-of-doors?
Across the echoless, stony floors
Into the windy corridors
The monks came flocking, and down the stair,
Silently, glancing each at each,
As if they had lost the power of speech.
Yes — it was some one knocking there!
And then — strange thing! — untouched by a soul
The bell of the convent 'gan to toll!
It curdled the blood beneath their hair.

Reaching the court, the brothers stood
Huddled together, pallid and mute,
By the massive door of iron-clamped wood,
Till one old monk, more resolute
Than the others — a man of pious will —
Stepped forth, and letting his lantern rest
On the pavement, crouched upon his breast

And peeped through a chink there was between
The cedar door and the sunken sill.
At the instant a flash of lightning came,
Seeming to wrap the world in flame.
He gave but a glance, and straight arose
With his face like a corpse's. What had he seen?
Two dripping, little pink-white toes!
Then, like a man gone suddenly wild,
He tugged at the bolts, flung down the chain,
And there, in the night and wind and rain —
Shivering, piteous, and forlorn,
And naked as ever it was born —
On the threshold stood the SAINTED CHILD!

"Since then," said Fra Gervasio,
"We have never let the Bambino go
Unwatched — no, not by a prince's bed.
Ah, signor, it made a dreadful stir."
"And the woman — Nina — what of her?
Had she no story?" He bowed his head,

And knitting his meagre fingers, so —
"In that night of wind and wrath," said he,
"There was wrought in Rome a mystery.
What know I, signor? They found her dead!"

ized by Google

IV.

INTERLUDES.

INTERLUDES.

DESTINY.

THREE roses, wan as moonlight and weighed down
    Each with its loveliness as with a crown,
Drooped in a florist's window in a town.

The first a lover bought. It lay at rest,
Like flower on flower, that night, on Beauty's breast.

The second rose, as virginal and fair,
Shrunk in the tangles of a harlot's hair.

The third, a widow, with new grief made wild,
Shut in the icy palm of her dead child.

UNSUNG.

As sweet as the breath that goes
From the lips of the white rose,
As weird as the elfin lights
That glimmer of frosty nights,
As wild as the winds that tear
The curled red leaf in the air,
Is the song I have never sung.

In slumber, a hundred times
I 've said the enchanted rhymes,
But ere I open my eyes
This ghost of a poem flies;
Of the interfluent strains
Not even a note remains:
I know by my pulses' beat
It was something wild and sweet,

UNSUNG.

And my heart is strangely stirred
By an unremembered word!

I strive, but I strive in vain,
To recall the lost refrain.
On some miraculous day
Perhaps it will come and stay;
In some unimagined Spring
I may find my voice, and sing
The song I have never sung.

FROST-WORK.

THESE winter nights, against my window-pane
    Nature with busy pencil draws designs
Of ferns and blossoms and fine spray of pines,
Oak-leaf and acorn and fantastic vines,
Which she will make when summer comes again —
Quaint arabesques in argent, flat and cold,
Like curious Chinese etchings . . . By and by,
Walking my leafy garden as of old,
These frosty fantasies shall charm my eye
In azure, damask, emerald, and gold.

ROCOCO.

BY studying my lady's eyes
    I've grown so learnéd day by day,
So Machiavelian in this wise,
That when I send her flowers, I say

To each small flower (no matter what,
Geranium, pink, or tuberose,
Syringa, or forget-me-not,
Or violet) before it goes:

"Be not triumphant, little flower,
When on her haughty heart you lie,
But modestly enjoy your hour:
She'll weary of you by and by."

LANDSCAPE.

TWILIGHT.

GAUNT shadows stretch along the hill;
    Cold clouds drift slowly west;
Soft flocks of vagrant snow-flakes fill
    The redwing's empty nest.

By sunken reefs the hoarse sea roars;
    Above the shelving sands,
Like skeletons the sycamores
    Uplift their wasted hands.

The air is full of hints of grief,
    Strange voices touched with pain —
The pathos of the falling leaf
    And rustling of the rain.

In yonder cottage shines a light,
    Far-gleaming like a gem —
Not fairer to the Rabbins' sight
    Was star of Bethlehem!

IDENTITY.

SOMEWHERE — in desolate wind-swept space —
    In Twilight-land — in No-man's-land —
Two hurrying Shapes met face to face,
    And bade each other stand.

"And who are you?" cried one, a-gape,
    Shuddering in the gloaming light.
"I know not," said the second Shape,
    "I only died last night!"

NOCTURNE.

ITALY.

UP to her chamber window
   A slight wire trellis goes,
And up this Romeo's ladder
   Clambers a bold white rose.

I lounge in the ilex shadows,
   I see the lady lean,
Unclasping her silken girdle,
   The curtain's folds between.

She smiles on her white-rose lover,
   She reaches out her hand
And helps him in at the window —
   I see it where I stand!

To her scarlet lip she holds him,
   And kisses him many a time —
Ah, me! it was he that won her
   Because he dared to climb!

A SNOW-FLAKE.

ONCE he sang of summer,
    Nothing but the summer;
Now he sings of winter,
Of winter bleak and drear:
Just because there's fallen
A snow-flake on his forehead,
He must go and fancy
'T is winter all the year!

ACROSS THE STREET.

WITH lash on cheek, she comes and goes;
    I watch her when she little knows:
I wonder if she dreams of it.
Sitting and working at my rhymes,
I weave into my verse at times
    Her sunny hair, or gleams of it.

Upon her window-ledge is set
A box of flowering mignonette;
    Morning and eve she tends to them —
The senseless flowers, that do not care
About that loosened strand of hair,
    As prettily she bends to them.

If I could once contrive to get
Into that box of mignonette

Some morning when she tends to them —
She comes! I see the rich blood rise
From throat to cheek! — down go the eyes,
Demurely, as she bends to them!

RENCONTRE.

TOILING across the Mer de Glace,
    I thought of, longed for thee;
What miles between us stretched, alas!—
    What miles of land and sea!

My foe, undreamed of, at my side
    Stood suddenly, like Fate.
For those who love, the world is wide,
    But not for those who hate.

AN UNTIMELY THOUGHT.

I WONDER what day of the week —
   I wonder what month of the year —
Will it be midnight, or morning,
   And who will bend over my bier?

— What a hideous fancy to come
   As I wait, at the foot of the stair,
While Lilian gives the last touch
   To her robe, or the rose in her hair.

Do I like your new dress — pompadour?
   And do I like *you*? On my life,
You are eighteen, and not a day more,
   And have not been six years my wife.

Those two rosy boys in the crib
   Up stairs are not ours, to be sure! —

You are just a sweet bride in her bloom,
All sunshine, and snowy, and pure.

As the carriage rolls down the dark street
The little wife laughs and makes cheer —
But . . . I wonder what day of the week,
I wonder what month of the year.

RONDEAU.

THE Summer comes and the Summer goes;
  Wild-flowers are fringing the dusty lanes,
    The swallows go darting through fragrant rains,
Then, all of a sudden — it snows.

Dear Heart, our lives so happily flow,
  So lightly we heed the flying hours,
    We only know Winter is gone — by the flowers,
We only know Winter is come — by the snow.

LATAKIA.

I.

WHEN all the panes are hung with frost,
    Wild wizard-work of silver lace,
I draw my sofa on the rug
Before the ancient chimney-place.

Upon the painted tiles are mosques
And minarets, and here and there
A blind muezzin lifts his hands
And calls the faithful unto prayer.

Folded in idle, twilight dreams,
I hear the hemlock chirp and sing
As if within its ruddy core
It held the happy heart of Spring.

Ferdousi never sang like that,
Nor Saadi grave, nor Hafiz gay:
I lounge, and blow white rings of smoke,
And watch them rise and float away.

II.

The curling wreaths like turbans seem
Of silent slaves that come and go —
Or Viziers, packed with craft and crime,
Whom I behead from time to time,
With pipe-stem, at a single blow.

And now and then a lingering cloud
Takes gracious form at my desire,
And at my side my lady stands,
Unwinds her veil with snowy hands —
A shadowy shape, a breath of fire!

O Love, if you were only here
Beside me in this mellow light,
Though all the bitter winds should blow,
And all the ways be choked with snow,
'T would be a true Arabian night!

A WINTER-PIECE.

> Sous le voile qui vous protége,
> Défiant les regards jaloux,
> Si vous sortez par cette neige,
> Redoutez vos pieds audalous.
> Théophile Gautier.

Beneath the heavy veil you wear,
    Shielded from jealous eyes you go;
But of your pretty feet have care
If you should venture through the snow.

Howe'er you tread, a dainty mould
Betrays that light foot all the same;
Upon this glistening, snowy fold
At every step it signs your name.

Thus guided, one might come too close
Upon the slyly-hidden nest
Where Psyche, with her cheek's cold rose,
On Love's warm bosom lies at rest.

QUATRAINS.

1.

DAY AND NIGHT.

Day is a snow-white Dove of heaven
    That from the East glad message brings:
Night is a stealthy, evil Raven,
    Wrapped to the eyes in his black wings.

2.

MAPLE LEAVES.

October turned my maple's leaves to gold;
The most are gone now; here and there one lingers:
Soon these will slip from out the twigs' weak hold,
Like coins between a dying miser's fingers.

3.

A CHILD'S GRAVE.

A LITTLE mound with chipped headstone,
The grass, ah me! uncut about the sward,
   Summer by summer left alone
With one white lily keeping watch and ward.

4.

PESSIMIST AND OPTIMIST.

THIS one sits shivering in Fortune's smile,
Taking his joy with bated, doubtful breath:
This other, gnawed by hunger, all the while
   Laughs in the teeth of Death.

5.

GRACE AND STRENGTH.

MANOAH'S son, in his blind rage malign,
   Tumbling the temple down upon his foes,
Did no such feat as yonder delicate vine
   That day by day untired holds up a rose.

6.

AMONG THE PINES.

FAINT murmurs from the pine-tops reach my ear,
As if a harpstring — touched in some far sphere —
Vibrating in the lucid atmosphere,
Let the soft south-wind waft its music here.

7.

FROM THE SPANISH.

To him that hath, we are told,
Shall be given. Yes, by the Cross!
To the rich man fate sends gold,
To the poor man loss on loss.

8.

MOONRISE AT SEA.

UP from the dark the moon begins to creep;
And now a pallid, haggard face lifts she
Above the water-line: thus from the deep
A drownéd body rises solemnly.

9.

MASKS.

Black Tragedy lets slip her grim disguise
And shows you laughing lips and roguish eyes;
But when, unmasked, gay Comedy appears,
'T is ten to one you find the girl in tears.

10.

COQUETTE.

Or light or dark, or short or tall,
She sets a springe to snare them all;
All 's one to her — above her fan
She 'd make sweet eyes at Caliban.

11.

EPITAPHS.

"Honest Iago." When his breath was fled
Doubtless these words were carven at his head.
Such lying epitaphs are like a rose
That in unlovely earth takes root and grows.

12.

POPULARITY.

Such kings of shreds have wooed and won her,
    Such crafty knaves her laurel owned,
It has become almost an honor
    Not to be crowned.

13.

HUMAN IGNORANCE.

What mortal knows
Whence come the tint and odor of the rose?
    What probing deep
Has ever solved the mystery of sleep?

14.

SPENDTHRIFT.

The fault's not mine, you understand:
    God shaped my palm so I can hold
But little water in my hand
    And not much gold.

15.

THE IRON AGE.

The big-lipped Sphinx, with bent perpléxéd brow,
Crouches in desert sand, inert and pale,
Hearing the engine's raucous scream, that now
Sends Echo flying through the Memphian vale.

16.

ON READING ——

Great thoughts in crude, inadequate verse set forth,
    Lose half their preciousness, and ever must.
    Unless the diamond with its own rich dust
Be cut and polished, it seems little worth.

17.

THE ROSE.

Fixed to her necklace, like another gem,
    A rose she wore — the flower June made for her;
Fairer it looked than when upon the stem,
    And must, indeed, have been much happier.

18.

FROM EASTERN SOURCES.

I.

In youth my hair was black as night,
   My life as white as driven snow:
   As white as snow my hair is now,
And that is black which once was white.

II.

No wonder Sajib wrote such verses, when
He had the bill of nightingale for pen;
   Or that his lyrics were divine
   Whose only ink was tears and wine.

III.

A poor dwarf's figure, looming through the dense
Mists of a mountain, seemed a shape immense,
On seeing which, a giant, in dismay,
   Took to his heels and ran away.

19.

THE PARCÆ.

In their dark House of Cloud
The three weird sisters toil till time be sped:
One unwinds life; one ever weaves the shroud;
One waits to cut the thread.

FABLE.

A CERTAIN bird in a certain wood,
  Feeling the spring-time warm and good,
Sang to it, in melodious mood.
On other neighboring branches stood
Other birds who heard his song:
Loudly he sang, and clear and strong;
Sweetly he sang, and it stirred their gall
There should be a voice so musical.
They said to themselves: "We must stop that bird,
He's the sweetest voice was ever heard.
That rich, deep chest-note, crystal-clear,
Is a mortifying thing to hear.
We have sharper beaks and hardier wings,
Yet we but croak: *this* fellow sings!"

So they planned and planned, and killed the bird
With the sweetest voice was ever heard.

Passing his grave one happy May,
I brought this English daisy away.

Rome, 1875.

PALINODE.

I.

When I was young and light of heart
I made sad songs with easy art:
Now I am sad, and no more young,
My sorrow cannot find a tongue.

II.

Pray, Muses, since I may not sing
Of Death or any grievous thing,
Teach me some joyous strain, that I
May mock my youth's hypocrisy!

V.

THE FLIGHT OF THE GODDESS, ETC.

THE FLIGHT OF THE GODDESS, ETC.

THE FLIGHT OF THE GODDESS.

A MAN should live in a garret aloof,
    And have few friends, and go poorly clad,
With an old hat stopping the chink in the roof,
To keep the Goddess constant and glad.

Of old, when I walked on a rugged way,
And gave much work for but little bread,
The Goddess dwelt with me night and day,
Sat at my table, haunted my bed.

The narrow, mean attic, I see it now! —
Its window o'erlooking the city's tiles,
The sunset's fires, and the clouds of snow,
And the river wandering miles and miles.

Just one picture hung in the room,
The saddest story that Art can tell —
Dante and Virgil in lurid gloom
Watching the Lovers float through Hell.

Wretched enough was I sometimes,
Pinched, and harassed with vain desires;
But thicker than clover sprung the rhymes
As I dwelt like a sparrow among the spires.

Midnight filled my slumbers with song;
Music haunted my dreams by day:
Now I listen and wait and long,
But the Delphian airs have died away.

I wonder and wonder how it befell:
Suddenly I had friends in crowds;
I bade the house-tops a long farewell;
"Good by," I cried, "to the stars and clouds!

THE FLIGHT OF THE GODDESS.

"But thou, rare soul, that hast dwelt with me,
Spirit of Poesy! thou divine
Breath of the morning, thou shalt be,
Goddess! for ever and ever mine."

And the woman I loved was now my bride,
And the house I wanted was my own;
I turned to the Goddess satisfied —
But the Goddess had somehow flown!

Flown, and I fear she will never return:
I am much too sleek and happy for her,
Whose lovers must hunger, and waste, and burn,
Ere the beautiful heathen heart will stir!

I call — but she does not stoop to my cry;
I wait — but she lingers, and ah! so long!
It was not so in the years gone by,
When she touched my lips with chrism of song.

I swear I will get me a garret again,
And adore, like a Parsee, the sunset's fires,
And lure the Goddess, by vigil and pain,
Up with the sparrows among the spires.

For a man should live in a garret aloof,
And have few friends, and go poorly clad,
With an old hat stopping the chink in the roof,
To keep the Goddess constant and glad.

ON AN INTAGLIO HEAD OF MINERVA.

BENEATH the warrior's helm, behold
　　The flowing tresses of the woman!
Minerva, Pallas, what you will—
　　A winsome creature, Greek or Roman.

Minerva? No! 'tis some sly minx
　　In cousin's helmet masquerading;
If not—then Wisdom was a dame
　　For sonnets and for serenading!

I thought the goddess cold, austere,
　　Not made for love's despairs and blisses:
Did Pallas wear her hair like that?
　　Was Wisdom's mouth so shaped for kisses?

The Nightingale should be her bird,
    And not the Owl, big-eyed and solemn:
How very fresh she looks, and yet
    She's older far than Trajan's Column!

The magic hand that carved this face,
    And set this vine-work round it running,
Perhaps ere mighty Phidias wrought
    Had lost its subtle skill and cunning.

Who was he? Was he glad or sad,
    Who knew to carve in such a fashion?
Perchance he graved the dainty head
    For some brown girl that scorned his passion.

Perchance, in some still garden-place,
    Where neither fount nor tree to-day is,
He flung the jewel at the feet
    Of Phryne, or perhaps 't was Laïs.

But he is dust; we may not know
   His happy or unhappy story:
Nameless, and dead these centuries,
   His work outlives him — there's his glory!

Both man and jewel lay in earth
   Beneath a lava-buried city;
The countless summers came and went
   With neither haste, nor hate, nor pity.

Years blotted out the man, but left
   The jewel fresh as any blossom,
Till some Visconti dug it up —
   To rise and fall on Mabel's bosom!

O nameless brother! see how Time
   Your gracious handiwork has guarded:
See how your loving, patient art
   Has come, at last, to be rewarded.

Who would not suffer slights of men,
    And pangs of hopeless passion also,
To have his carven agate-stone
    On such a bosom rise and fall so!

THE GUERDON.

SOOTHED by the fountain's drowsy murmuring —
  Or was it by the west-wind's indolent wing ? —
The grim court-poet fell asleep one day
In the lords' chamber, when chance brought that way
The Princess Margaret with a merry train
Of damozels and ladies — flippant, vain
Court-butterflies — midst whom fair Margaret
Swayed like a rathe and slender lily set
In rustling leaves, for all her drapery
Was green and gold, and lovely as could be.

  Midway in hall the fountain rose and fell,
Filling a listless Naiad's outstretched shell
And weaving rainbows in the shifting light.
Upon the carven friezes, left and right,

Was pictured Pan asleep beside his reed.

In this place all things seemed asleep, indeed —

The hook-billed parrot on his pendent ring,

Sitting high-shouldered, half forgot to swing;

The wind scarce stirred the hangings at the door,

And from the silken arras evermore

Yawned drowsy dwarfs with satyr's face and hoof.

A forest of gold pillars propped the roof,

And like one slim gold pillar overthrown,

The sunlight through a great stained window shone

And lay across the body of Alain.

You would have thought, perchance, the man was slain:

As if the checkered column in its fall

Had caught and crushed him, he lay dead to all.

The parrot's gray bead eye as good as said,

Unclosing viciously, "The clown is dead."

A dragon-fly in narrowing circles neared,

And lit, secure, upon the dead man's beard,

Then spread its iris vans in quick dismay,

And into the blue summer sped away!

THE GUERDON.

Little was his of outward grace to win
The eyes of maids, but white the soul within.
Misshaped, and hideous to look upon
Was this man, dreaming in the noontide sun,
With sunken eyes and winter-whitened hair,
And sallow cheeks deep seamed with thought and care.
And so the laughing ladies of the court,
Coming upon him suddenly, stopped short,
And shrunk together with a nameless dread;
Some, but fear held them, would have turned and fled,
Seeing the uncouth figure lying there.
But Princess Margaret, with her heavy hair
From out its diamond fillet rippling down,
Slipped from the group, and plucking back her gown
With white left hand, stole softly to his side —
The fair court gossips staring, curious-eyed,
Half mockingly. A little while she stood,
Finger on lip; then, with the agile blood
Climbing her cheek, and silken lashes wet —
She scarce knew what vague pity or regret
Wet them — she stooped, and for a moment's space

Her golden tresses touched the sleeper's face.
Then she stood straight, as lily on its stem,
But hearing her ladies titter, turned on them
Her great queen's eyes, grown black with scornful
    frown —
Great eyes that looked the shallow women down.
"Nay, not for love" — one rosy palm she laid
Softly against her bosom — "as I'm a maid!
Full well I know what cruel things you say
Of this and that, but hold your peace to-day.
I pray you think no evil thing of this.
Nay, not for love's sake did I give the kiss,
Not for his beauty who's nor fair nor young,
But for the songs which those mute lips have sung!"

That was a right brave princess, one, I hold,
Worthy to wear a crown of beaten gold.

LOST AT SEA.

THE face that Carlo Dolci drew
   Looks down from out its leafy hood —
The holly berries, gleaming through
The pointed leaves, seem drops of blood.

Above the cornice, round the hearth,
Are evergreens and spruce-tree boughs;
'T is Christmas morning: Christmas mirth
And joyous voices fill the house.

I pause, and know not what to do;
I feel reproach that I am glad:
Until to-day, no thought of you,
O Comrade! ever made me sad.

But now the thought of your blithe heart,
Your ringing laugh, can give me pain,
Knowing that we are worlds apart,
Not knowing we shall meet again.

For all is dark that lies in store:
Though they may preach, the brotherhood,
We know just this, and nothing more,
That we are dust, and God is good.

What life begins when death makes end?
Sleek gownsman, is 't so very clear?
How fares it with us? — O, my Friend,
I only know you are not here!

That I am in a warm, light room,
With life and love to comfort me,
While you are drifting through the gloom,
Beneath the sea, beneath the sea!

O wild green waves that lash the sands
Of Santiago and beyond,
Lift him, I pray, with gentle hands,
And bear him on — true heart and fond!

To some still grotto far below
The washings of the warm Gulf Stream
Bear him, and let the winds that blow
About the world not break his dream!

— I smooth my brow. Upon the stair
I hear my children shout in glee,
With sparkling eyes and floating hair,
Bringing a Christmas wreath for me.

Their joy, like sunshine deep and broad,
Falls on my heart, and makes me glad:
I think the face of our dear Lord
Looks down on them, and seems not sad.

AN OLD CASTLE.

I.

THE gray arch crumbles,
    And totters, and tumbles;
The bat has built in the banquet hall.
In the donjon-keep
Sly mosses creep;
The ivy has scaled the southern wall.
No man-at-arms
Sounds quick alarms
A-top of the cracked martello tower.
The drawbridge-chain
Is broken in twain;
The bridge will neither rise nor lower.
Not any manner
Of broidered banner

Flaunts at a blazoned herald's call.

Lilies float

In the stagnant moat;

And fair they are, and tall.

II.

Here, in the old

Forgotten springs,

Was wassail held by queens and kings;

Here at the board

Sat clown and lord,

Maiden fair and lover bold,

Baron fat and minstrel lean,

The prince with his stars,

The knight with his scars,

The priest in his gabardine.

III.

Where is she

Of the fleur-de-lys,

And that true knight who wore her gages?

Where are the glances
That bred wild fancies
In curly heads of my lady's pages?
Where are those
Who, in steel or hose,
Held revel here, and made them gay?
Where is the laughter
That shook the rafter —
Where is the rafter, by the way?
Gone is the roof,
And perched aloof
Is an owl, like a friar of Orders Gray.
(Perhaps 't is the priest
Come back to feast —
He had ever a tooth for capon, he!
But the capon's cold,
And the steward's old,
And the butler's lost the larder-key!)

The doughty lords
Sleep the sleep of swords.

Dead are the dames and damozels.
The King in his crown
Hath laid him down,
And the Jester with his bells.

IV.

All is dead here:
Poppies are red here,
Vines in my lady's chamber grow —
If 't was her chamber
Where they clamber
Up from the poisonous weeds below.
All is dead here,
Joy is fled here;
Let us hence. 'T is the end of all —
The gray arch crumbles,
And totters, and tumbles,
And Silence sits in the banquet hall.

IN AN ATELIER.

I PRAY you, do not turn your head;
   And let your hands lie folded, so.
It was a dress like this, wine-red,
That Dante liked so, long ago.
You don't know Dante? Never mind.
He loved a lady wondrous fair—
His model? Something of the kind.
I wonder if she had your hair!

I wonder if she looked so meek,
And was not meek at all (my dear,
I want that side light on your cheek).
He loved her, it is very clear,
And painted her, as I paint you,
But rather better, on the whole

(Depress your chin; yes, that will do):
He was a painter of the soul!

(And painted portraits, too, I think,
In the INFERNO — devilish good!
I'd make some certain critics blink
If I'd his method and his mood.)
Her name was (Fanny, let your glance
Rest there, by that majolica tray) —
Was Beatrice; they met by chance —
They met by chance, the usual way.

(As you and I met, months ago,
Do you remember? How your feet
Went crinkle-crinkle on the snow
Along the bleak gas-lighted street!
An instant in the drug-store's glare
You stood as in a golden frame,
And then I swore it, then and there,
To hand your sweetness down to fame.)

They met, and loved, and never wed
(All this was long before our time),
And though they died, they are not dead —
Such endless youth gives mortal rhyme!
Still walks the earth, with haughty mien,
Great Dante, in his soul's distress;
And still the lovely Florentine
Goes lovely in her wine-red dress.

You do not understand at all?
He was a poet; on his page
He drew her; and, though kingdoms fall,
This lady lives from age to age:
A poet — that means painter too,
For words are colors, rightly laid;
And they outlast our brightest hue,
For varnish cracks and crimsons fade.

The poets — they are lucky ones!
When *we* are thrust upon the shelves,
Our works turn into skeletons

Almost as quickly as ourselves;
For our poor canvas peels at length,
At length is prized — when all is bare:
"What grace!" the critics cry, "what strength!"
When neither strength nor grace is there.

Ah, Fanny, I am sick at heart,
It is so little one can do;
We talk our jargon — live for Art!
I'd much prefer to live for you.
How dull and lifeless colors are!
You smile, and all my picture lies:
I wish that I could crush a star
To make a pigment for your eyes.

Yes, child, I know I'm out of tune;
The light is bad; the sky is gray:
I'll paint no more this afternoon,
So lay your royal gear away.
Besides, you're moody — chin on hand —
I know not what — not in the vein —

Not Anne Bullen, sweet and bland:
You sit there looking like Elaine.

Not like Bluff Harry's radiant Queen,
Unconscious of the coming woe,
But rather as she might have been,
Preparing for the headsman's blow.
I see! I've put you in a miff —
Sitting bolt-upright, wrist on wrist.
How *should* you look? Why, dear, as if —
Somehow — as if you'd just been kissed!

THE WORLD'S WAY.

AT Haroun's court it chanced, upon a time,
An Arab poet made this pleasant rhyme:

"The new moon is a horseshoe, wrought of God,
Wherewith the Sultan's stallion shall be shod." [1]

On hearing this, his highness smiled, and gave
The man a gold-piece. *Sing again, O slave!*

Above his lute the happy singer bent,
And turned another gracious compliment.

And, as before, the smiling Sultan gave
The man a sekkah. *Sing again, O slave!*

[1] Variation of a couplet in Alger's "Poetry of the East."

Again the verse came, fluent as a rill
That wanders, silver-footed, down a hill.

The Sultan, listening, nodded as before,
Still gave the gold, and still demanded more.

The nimble fancy that had climbed so high
Grew weary with its climbing by and by:

Strange discords rose; the sense went quite amiss;
The singer's rhymes refused to meet and kiss:

Invention flagged, the lute had got unstrung,
And twice he sang the song already sung.

The Sultan, furious, called a mute, and said,
O Musta, straightway whip me off his head!

Poets! not in Arabia alone
You get beheaded when your skill is gone.

TITA'S TEARS.

A FANTASY.

A CERTAIN man of Ischia — it is thus
  The story runs — one Lydus Claudius,
After a life of threescore years and ten,
Passed suddenly from out the world of men
Into the world of shadows.
                              In a vale
Where shoals of spirits against the moonlight pale
Surged ever upward, in a wan-lit place
Near heaven, he met a Presence face to face —
A figure like a carving on a spire,
Shrouded in wings and with a fillet of fire
About the brows — who stayed him there, and said:
"This the gods grant to thee, O newly dead!
Whatever thing on earth thou holdest dear

Shall, at thy bidding, be transported here,
Save wife or child, or any living thing."
Then straightway Claudius fell to wondering
What he should wish for. Having heaven at hand,
His wants were few, as you can understand.
Riches and titles, matters dear to us,
To him, of course, were now superfluous:
But Tita, small brown Tita, his young wife,
A two weeks' bride when he took leave of life,
What would become of her without his care?
Tita, so rich, so thoughtless, and so fair!
At present crushed with sorrow, to be sure —
But by and by? What earthly griefs endure?
They pass like joys. A year, three years at most,
And would she mourn her lord, so quickly lost?
With fine, prophetic ear, he heard afar
The tinkling of some horrible guitar
Under her balcony. "Such thing could be,"
Sighed Claudius; "I would she were with me,
Safe from all harm." But as that wish was vain,
He let it drift from out his troubled brain

(His highly trained austerity was such
That self-denial never cost him much),
And strove to think what object he might name
Most closely linked with the bereavéd dame.
Her wedding ring? — 't would be too small to wear;
Perhaps a ringlet of her raven hair?
If not, her portrait, done in cameo,
Or on a background of pale gold? But no,
Such trifles jarred with his severity.
At length he thought: "The thing most meet for me
Would be that antique flask wherein my bride
Let fall her heavy tears the night I died."
(It was a custom of that simple day
To have one's tears sealed up and laid away,
As everlasting tokens of regret —
They find the bottles in Greek ruins yet.)
For this he wished, then.

      Swifter than a thought
The Presence vanished, and the flask was brought —
Slender, bell-mouthed, and painted all around
With jet-black tulips on a saffron ground;

TITA'S TEARS.

A tiny jar, of porcelain if you will,
Which twenty tears would rather more than fill.
With careful fingers Claudius broke the seal
When, suddenly, a well-known merry peal
Of laughter leapt from out the vial's throat,
And died, as dies the wood-bird's distant note.
Claudius stared; then, struck with strangest fears,
Reversed the flask —
    Alas, for Tita's tears!

THE KING'S WINE.

THE small green grapes in countless clusters grew,
    Feeding on mystic moonlight and white dew
And mellow sunshine, the long summer through:

Till, with faint tremor in her veins, the vine
Felt the delicious pulses of the wine;
And the grapes ripened in the year's decline.

And day by day the Virgins watched their charge;
And when, at last, beyond the horizon's marge,
The harvest moon drooped beautiful and large,

The subtile spirit in the grape was caught,
And to the slowly dying monarch brought
In a great cup fantastically wrought.

Of this he drank; then straightway from his brain
Went the weird malady, and once again
He walked the Palace, free of scar or pain—

But strangely changed, for somehow he had lost
Body and voice: the courtiers, as he crossed
The royal chambers, whispered — *The King's ghost!*

DIRGE.

LET us keep him warm,
   Stir the dying fire:
Upon his tired arm
Slumbers young Desire.

Soon, ah, very soon
We too shall not know
Either sun or moon,
Either grass or snow.

Others in our place
Come to laugh and weep,
Win or lose the race,
And to fall asleep.

Let us keep him warm,
Stir the dying fire:
Upon his tired arm
Slumbers young Desire.

What does all avail —
Love, or power, or gold?
Life is like a tale
Ended ere 't is told.

Much is left unsaid,
Much is said in vain —
Shall the broken thread
Be taken up again?

Let us keep him warm,
Stir the dying fire:
Upon his tired arm
Slumbers young Desire.

Kisses one or two
On his eyelids set,
That, when all is through,
He may not forget.

He has far to go —
Is it East or West?
Whither? Who may know!
Let him take his rest.

Wind, and snow, and sleet —
So the long night dies.
Draw the winding-sheet,
Cover up his eyes.

Let us keep him warm,
Stir the dying fire:
Upon his tired arm
Slumbers young Desire.

THE PIAZZA OF ST. MARK AT MIDNIGHT.

HUSHED is the music, hushed the hum of voices;
   Gone is the crowd of dusky promenaders —
Slender-waisted, almond-eyed Venetians,
Princes and paupers. Not a single footfall
Sounds in the arches of the Procuratie.
One after one, like sparks in cindered paper,
Faded the lights out in the goldsmiths' windows.
Drenched with the moonlight lies the still Piazza.

Fair as the palace builded for Aladdin,
Yonder St. Mark uplifts its sculptured splendor —
Intricate fretwork, Byzantine mosaic,
Color on color, column upon column,
Barbaric, wonderful, a thing to kneel to!
Over the portal stand the four gilt horses,

Gilt hoof in air, and wide distended nostril,
Fiery, untamed, as in the days of Nero.
Skyward, a cloud of domes and spires and crosses;
Earthward, black shadows flung from jutting stone-work.
High over all the slender Campanile
Quivers, and seems a falling shaft of silver!

Hushed is the music, hushed the hum of voices.
From coigne and cornice and fantastic gargoyle,
At intervals the moan of dove or pigeon,
Fairily faint, floats off into the moonlight.
This, and the murmur of the Adriatic,
Lazily restless, lapping the mossed marble,
Staircase or buttress, scarcely break the stillness.
Deeper each moment seems to grow the silence,
Denser the moonlight in the still Piazza.
Hark! on the Tower above the ancient gateway,
The twin bronze Vulcans, with their ponderous hammers,
Hammer the midnight on their brazen bell there!

THORWALDSEN.

WE often fail by searching far and wide
   For what lies close at hand. To serve our turn
We ask fair wind and favorable tide.
From the dead Danish sculptor let us learn
To make Occasion, not to be denied:
Against the sheer, precipitous mountain-side
Thorwaldsen carved his Lion at Lucerne.

VI.

SONNETS.

SONNETS.

"EVEN THIS WILL PASS AWAY."

TOUCHED with the delicate green of early May,
   Or later, when the rose unveils her face,
   The world hangs glittering in star-strown space,
   Fresh as a jewel found but yesterday.
And yet 't is very old; what tongue may say
   How old it is? Race follows upon race,
   Forgetting and forgotten; in their place
   Sink tower and temple; nothing long may stay.
We build on tombs, and live our day, and die;
   From out our dust new towers and temples start;
   Our very name becomes a mystery.
What cities no man ever heard of lie
   Under the glacier, in the mountain's heart,
   In violet glooms beneath the moaning sea!

AT STRATFORD-UPON-AVON.

TO EDWIN BOOTH.

THUS spake his dust (so seemed it as I read
    The words): *Good frend, for Jesus' sake forbeare*
(Poor ghost!) *To digg the dvst enclosèd heare* —
Then came the malediction on the head
Of who so dare disturb the sacred dead.
    Outside the mavis whistled strong and clear,
    And, touched with the sweet glamour of the year,
    The winding Avon murmured in its bed.
But in the solemn Stratford church the air
    Was chill and dank, and on the foot-worn tomb
    The evening shadows deepened momently:
Then a great awe crept on me, standing there,
    As if some speechless Presence in the gloom
    Was hovering, and fain would speak with me.

THREE FLOWERS.

TO BAYARD TAYLOR.

HEREWITH I send you three pressed withered
    flowers:
This one was white, with golden star; this, blue
As Capri's cave; that, purple and shot through
With sunset-orange. Where the Duomo towers
In diamond air, and under hanging bowers
  The Arno glides, this faded violet grew
  On Landor's grave; from Landor's heart it drew
  Its magic azure in the long spring hours.
Within the shadow of the Pyramid
  Of Caius Cestius was the daisy found,
    White as the soul of Keats in Paradise.
The pansy — there were hundreds of them, hid
  In the thick grass that folded Shelley's mound,
    Guarding his ashes with most lovely eyes.

AN ALPINE PICTURE.

STAND here and look, and softly hold your breath
   Lest the vast avalanche come crashing down!
How many miles away is yonder town
   Set flower-wise in the valley? Far beneath —
A scimitar half drawn from out its sheath —
   The river curves through meadows newly mown;
The ancient water-courses are all strown
   With drifts of snow, fantastic wreath on wreath;
And peak on peak against the turquoise-blue
   The Alps like towering campanili stand,
     Wondrous, with pinnacles of frozen rain,
Silvery, crystal, like the prism in hue.
   O tell me, Love, if this be Switzerland —
     Or is it but the frost-work on the pane?

TO LAUNT THOMPSON IN FLORENCE.

YOU by the Arno shape your marble dream,
   Under the cypress and the olive trees,
  While I, this side the wild, wind-beaten seas,
  Unrestful by the Charles's placid stream,
Long once again to catch the golden gleam
   Of Brunelleschi's dome, and lounge at ease
  In those pleached gardens and fair galleries.
  And yet, perhaps, you envy me, and deem
My star the happier, since it holds me here.
  Even so, one time, beneath the cypresses
   My heart turned longingly across the sea,
Aching with love for thee, New England dear!
  And I'd have given all Titian's goddesses
   For one poor cowslip or anemone.

ENGLAND.

WHILE men pay reverence to mighty things,
    They must revere thee, thou blue-cinctured isle
Of England — not to-day, but this long while
In the front of nations, Mother of great kings,
Soldiers, and poets. Round thee the Sea flings
    His steel-bright arm, and shields thee from the guile
And hurt of France. Secure, with august smile,
Thou sittest, and the East its tribute brings.
Some say thy old-time power is on the wane,
    Thy moon of grandeur filled, contracts at length —
    They see it darkening down from less to less.
Let but a hostile hand make threat again,
    And they shall see thee in thy ancient strength,
    Each iron sinew quivering, lioness!

ENAMORED ARCHITECT OF AIRY RHYME.

ENAMORED architect of airy rhyme,
  Build as thou wilt; heed not what each man says.
  Good souls, but innocent of dreamers' ways,
  Will come, and marvel why thou wastest time;
Others, beholding how thy turrets climb
  'Twixt theirs and heaven, will hate thee all their days;
  But most beware of those who come to praise.
  O Wondersmith, O worker in sublime
And heaven-sent dreams, let art be all in all;
  Build as thou wilt, unspoiled by praise or blame,
    Build as thou wilt, and as thy light is given:
Then, if at last the airy structure fall,
  Dissolve, and vanish — take thyself no shame.
    They fail, and they alone, who have not striven.

HENRY HOWARD BROWNELL.

THEY never crowned him, never knew his worth,
    But let him go unlaurelled to the grave:
  Hereafter there are guerdons for the brave,
  Roses for martyrs who wear thorns on earth,
Balms for bruised hearts that languish in the dearth
  Of human love. So let the lilies wave
  Above him, nameless. Little did he crave
  Men's praises. Modestly, with kindly mirth,
Not sad nor bitter, he accepted fate —
  Drank deep of life, knew books, and hearts of men,
    Cities and camps, and war's immortal woe,
Yet bore through all (such virtue in him sate
  His Spirit is not whiter now than then!)
    A simple, loyal nature, pure as snow.

BARBERRIES.

IN scarlet clusters o'er the gray stone-wall
    The barberries lean in thin autumnal air:
Just when the fields and garden-plots are bare,
And ere the green leaf takes the tint of fall,
They come, to make the eye a festival!
    Along the road, for miles, their torches flare.
    Ah, if your deep-sea coral were but rare
(The damask rose might envy it withal),
What bards had sung your praises long ago,
    Called you fine names in honey-worded books —
    The rosy tramps of turnpike and of lane,
September's blushes, Ceres' lips aglow,
    Little Red-Ridinghoods, for your sweet looks! —
    But your plebeian beauty is in vain.

THE LORELEI.

A RHINE LEGEND.

YONDER we see it from the steamer's deck,
  The haunted Mountain of the Lorelei —
  The o'erhanging crags sharp-cut against a sky
  Clear as a sapphire without flaw or fleck.
'T was here the Siren lay in wait to wreck
  The fisher-lad. At dusk, as he passed by,
  Perchance he 'd hear her tender amorous sigh,
  And, seeing the wondrous whiteness of her neck,
Perchance would halt, and lean towards the shore;
  Then she by that soft magic which she had
    Would lure him, and in gossamers of her hair,
Gold upon gold, would wrap him o'er and o'er,
  Wrap him, and sing to him, and set him mad,
    Then drag him down to no man knoweth where.

THE RARITY OF GENIUS.

WHILE yet my lip was breathing youth's first breath,
  Too young to feel the utmost of their spell
  I saw Medea and Phædra in Rachel:
  Later I saw the great Elizabeth.
Rachel, Ristori — we shall taste of death
  Ere we meet spirits like these: in one age dwell
  Not many such; a century may tell
  Its hundred beads before it braid a wreath
For two so queenly foreheads. If it take
  Æons to form a diamond, grain on grain,
    Æons to crystallize its fire and dew —
By what slow processes must Nature make
  Her Shakespeares and her Raffaels? Great the gain
    If she spoil thousands making one or two.

SLEEP.

WHEN to soft Sleep we give ourselves away,
    And in a dream as in a fairy bark
    Drift on and on through the enchanted dark
    To purple daybreak — little thought we pay
To that sweet bitter world we know by day.
    We are clean quit of it, as is a lark
    So high in heaven no human eye may mark
    The thin swift pinion cleaving through the gray.
Till we awake ill fate can do no ill,
    The resting heart shall not take up again
      The heavy load that yet must make it bleed;
For this brief space the loud world's voice is still,
    No faintest echo of it brings us pain.
      How will it be when we shall sleep indeed?

TAKE them and keep them,
    Silvery thorn and flower,
Plucked just at random
    In the rosy weather —
Snowdrops and pansies,
    Sprigs of wayside heather,
And five-leaved wild-rose
    Dead within an hour.

Take them and keep them:
    Who can tell? some day, dear,
(Though they be withered,
    Flower and thorn and blossom,)
Held for an instant
    Up against thy bosom,
They might make December
    Seem to thee like May, dear!

www.ingramcontent.com/pod-product-compliance
Lightning Source LLC
Chambersburg PA
CBHW020056170426
43199CB00009B/297